HOME

A JOURNAL

PLANS, TIPS, AND PROMPTS
FOR CREATING YOUR FOREVER HOME

THE KHALIGHIS

wellfleet
press

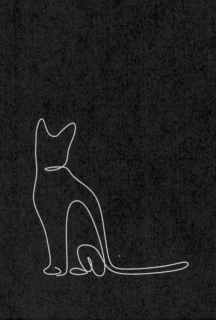

For Minnow and Dorito

and all furry, fluffy, feathered, and scaly family members

who make every house a home.

CONTENTS

Introduction

WHAT TURNS A HOUSE INTO A HOME?
It could very well be the foundation, literally and figuratively.

House building 101: A structure should have a solid starting point with land that is sturdy, unflexing, and able to withstand all the elements and potential natural disasters. The materials used should be just as strong, reliable, and able to protect the precious contents within for years to come.

This very simple description of how to build a house is very much like how one might go about creating a home. The matriarch or patriarch with all their memories, values, and beliefs, providing guidance and support to the rest of the family, acts as the foundation, and the additional materials that come together to further strengthen the initial structure are our dear friends, pets, and other family members, both chosen and related.

Laying the foundation—whether that means literally putting down concrete slabs or making house rules and creating mantras and traditions for your family—is the beginning of everything and the most important step on the path from house to home. All the furniture, décor, and paint in the world will do nothing to enhance your home if the emotional connection to it is absent. As it is said, all roads lead to home, so in establishing this foundation, you are creating the center of your whole world.

Most importantly, your home *is* you. It's a reflection of all your journeys and experiences that have come together to create a space that is wholly your happy place. As others pass through, they will leave bits of themselves behind, which will only level up your space with good vibes and deep feelings.

So, what turns a house into a home? That's entirely up to you.

"The sun at home warms better than the sun elsewhere."
—Albanian Wisdom

How to Use This Book

HOME IS A COMBINATION JOURNAL, workbook, and record keeper, a multipurpose sidekick for the journey of your home. Its portable size and durable nature are intentional so that you can feel comfortable taking it along wherever your adventures take you, from the worksite to the lumberyard and beyond. Additionally, _Home_ is meant to be a keepsake, one that can be put on display, added to, and updated for years to come.

Parts I and II are for you to chronicle your experiences around how you came to find your home and what you've learned once you've dug into its history and that of the surrounding areas. Part III is for recording all your memories with family and friends, new traditions you've made, and all the special moments spent at home. Parts IV and V are where things start to really get fun—this is where you note all your design inspiration and plans for your space, as well as track the progress of all your projects. _Home_ concludes with the practical part VI, where you can store all the important information for your home in one central location: appliance records, tax information, emergency contacts, and anything else that will help keep your home in working order.

A WORD ABOUT SAFETY

For all projects, no matter how small or large, safety is nonnegotiable. The DIY lifestyle is fun and exciting, but not if you have no idea what you're doing, so step one for each and every project you choose to take on yourself should be research.

Many contractors and tradespeople have their own video channels and blogs where they walk you through all the nuances of their projects. From tool and material recommendations to step-by-step tutorials and before and after shots, these experts are valuable resources for anyone looking to be hands-on in their home projects. Even if it's just painting, there are thousands of great options available through a simple internet search to instruct you on how to get those oh-so-desirable crisp, clean lines.

Making sure you are kitted up to take on these projects is just as vital. Don't disregard the importance of wearing the proper clothes and shoes. It is imperative that you also consider things like eye, ear, and head protection, as well as gloves and masks.

It's also important to be able to accept when a project is out of your comfort zone or beyond your skill level or abilities. That's when you call in the professionals. Take your time to research their previous work to make sure who you hire can execute your vision flawlessly, and _always_ get multiple quotes for projects, no fewer than three.

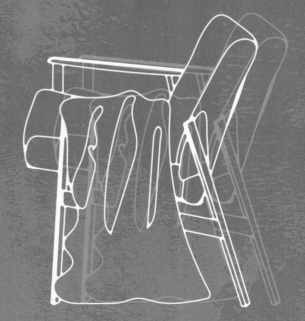

PART I

The Road
to Home

THE ROAD TO HOME

"If light is in your heart, you will find your way home."
—Rumi (1207–1273), Persian poet

ONE OF THE MOST REWARDING AND FUN EVENTS in a person's life is shopping for and eventually buying or renting their first home. Whether you're newly out on your own and living in a rental apartment or diving into your full-size homeowner adventure, the feeling of getting to make a space all your own is unmatched. But as exciting as the search can be, it is not always a stress-free experience. That is why being prepared, armed with information, and surrounded by an amazing support system is vital during such an important life event.

In this opening section you'll find everything you need to take you from dreaming to closing to moving in. When you start your search, it's an important exercise to visualize and record everything you could possibly want in your dream home, and then organize that list into needs versus wants. Some things are inevitably must-haves and would be deal breakers if they are absent from your space, while others would be nice-to-haves eventually, but maybe not this first time around.

From your realtor to your real estate attorney, pick people you feel comfortable with and, more importantly, whom you trust to advise you well and be in your corner during the whole process. Because this journey can be overwhelming, it's helpful to keep all your thoughts and important numbers organized and in one place, so here you will find space to log your impressions of all the places you see, all the offers you make, and any counteroffers you may receive. Keep the theme of organization going after closing as you prep and pack for the move. And once you've finally arrived in your new space (yay!), make sure everything and everyone important to you finds their way home with your address change and new address checklists.

Your Dream Home

Needs vs. Wants

NEEDS

WANTS

The Players

MY AGENT

NAME

OFFICE/FIRM NAME

ADDRESS

PHONE   EMAIL

SELLER'S AGENT/LANDLORD/MANAGEMENT COMPANY

NAME

OFFICE/FIRM NAME

ADDRESS

PHONE   EMAIL

MY REAL ESTATE ATTORNEY

NAME

OFFICE/FIRM NAME

ADDRESS

PHONE   EMAIL

SELLER'S REAL ESTATE ATTORNEY

NAME

OFFICE/FIRM NAME

ADDRESS

PHONE   EMAIL

TIP Not all areas require buyers or sellers to hire real estate attorneys, but they can add value by protecting your interests when dealing with pushy agents who just want to close the deal, and will stand up for you if they sense you may be taken advantage of by the other party.

HOME INSPECTOR

NAME

OFFICE/FIRM NAME

ADDRESS

PHONE   EMAIL

HOME APPRAISER

NAME

OFFICE/FIRM NAME

ADDRESS

PHONE   EMAIL

MORTGAGE COMPANY/BANK

NAME

OFFICE/FIRM NAME

ADDRESS

PHONE   EMAIL

TITLE AGENCY

NAME

OFFICE/FIRM NAME

ADDRESS

PHONE   EMAIL

FACT Realtors, brokers, agents, and loan officers are regulated professionals and must operate within a strict set of laws. Make sure you understand the differences between them and what their roles are so that you can ensure their interests align with yours throughout the buying process.

Open House Log

DATE SEEN   ASKING PRICE

....

....

ADDRESS

....

PROS

....

....

....

....

....

CONS

....

....

....

....

....

NOTES

....

....

....

....

DATE SEEN

ASKING PRICE

ADDRESS

PROS

CONS

NOTES

Open House Log

DATE SEEN

ASKING PRICE

ADDRESS

PROS

CONS

NOTES

DATE SEEN

ASKING PRICE

ADDRESS

PROS

CONS

NOTES

Open House Log

DATE SEEN

ASKING PRICE

....

....

ADDRESS

....

....

PROS

....

....

....

....

....

CONS

....

....

....

....

....

NOTES

....

....

....

....

DATE SEEN   ASKING PRICE
....
....

ADDRESS
....

PROS
....
....
....
....
....

CONS
....
....
....
....
....

NOTES
....
....
....
....

Open House Log

DATE SEEN

ASKING PRICE

....

....

ADDRESS

....

....

PROS

....

....

....

....

....

CONS

....

....

....

....

....

NOTES

....

....

....

....

DATE SEEN

ASKING PRICE

ADDRESS

PROS

CONS

NOTES

Open House Log

DATE SEEN   ASKING PRICE

....

....

ADDRESS

....

....

PROS

....

....

....

....

....

CONS

....

....

....

....

....

NOTES

....

....

....

....

DATE SEEN

ASKING PRICE

....

....

....

ADDRESS

....

....

PROS

....

....

....

....

....

....

CONS

....

....

....

....

....

....

NOTES

....

....

....

....

....

Offer Tracker

LOCATION

OFFER 1   DATE

COUNTEROFFER 1   DATE

OFFER 2   DATE

COUNTEROFFER 2   DATE

OFFER 3   DATE

COUNTEROFFER 3   DATE

NOTES

LOCATION

OFFER 1   DATE

COUNTEROFFER 1   DATE

OFFER 2   DATE

COUNTEROFFER 2   DATE

OFFER 3   DATE

COUNTEROFFER 3   DATE

NOTES

DID YOU KNOW?

Multiple hard credit checks within thirty days will typically count as one on your credit report.
This is to allow you to shop around for the best rate and terms for your loan without negatively
impacting your credit score.

Offer Tracker

LOCATION

....

OFFER 1   DATE

....

COUNTEROFFER 1   DATE

....

OFFER 2   DATE

....

COUNTEROFFER 2   DATE

....

OFFER 3   DATE

....

COUNTEROFFER 3   DATE

....

NOTES

....

....

....

....

....

....

....

....

....

LOCATION

....

OFFER 1   DATE
....

COUNTEROFFER 1   DATE
....

OFFER 2   DATE
....

COUNTEROFFER 2   DATE
....

OFFER 3   DATE
....

COUNTEROFFER 3   DATE
....

NOTES
....

....

....

....

....

....

TIP

Take the opportunity to shadow your home inspector during the home inspection process. They will show you the quirks and features of the house, so you can learn about the maintenance items to look out for and locate important features, such as electric and water shutoffs. You want to know where these are *before* you need them.

Closing Log

FINAL OFFER   **SALE DATE**

NOTES

FINAL WALK-THROUGH DATE

NOTES

CLOSING DATE

PARTIES PRESENT

NOTES

CLOSING COSTS

MOVE-IN DATE

Closing Log

FINAL OFFER   **SALE DATE**

NOTES

FINAL WALK-THROUGH DATE

NOTES

CLOSING DATE

PARTIES PRESENT

CLOSING COSTS

MOVE-IN DATE

TIP

Title insurance is an optional one-time purchase available during closing that protects the buyer in the event that an issue is found with the title of the property after closing. Consider buying it if there may be potential issues with the seller's ability to actually sell the home, such as when multiple parties have a legal claim to the home you are trying to buy—a divorce, a disputed inheritance—or unpaid contractors have opened liens against the title for completed work. Title insurance will help cover the legal costs to resolve these matters.

Moving To-Do List

Moving To-Do List

Packing List for

-
-
-
-
-
-
-
-
-

Packing List for

-
-
-
-
-
-
-
-
-

Packing List for ....

- ....
....

- ....
....

- ....
....

- ....
....

- ....
....

- ....
....

- ....
....

- ....
....

- ....
....

Packing List for ....

-
-
-
-
-
-
-
-
-

Packing List for

-
-
-
-
-
-
-
-
-

Packing List for

-
-
-
-
-
-
-
-
-

Packing List for

-
-
-
-
-
-
-
-

Packing List for

-
-
-
-
-
-
-
-
-

Address Change Checklist

	IMMEDIATE FAMILY
	EXTENDED FAMILY
	FRIENDS
	COWORKERS
	WORKPLACE HR/AP
	BANK/FINANCIAL INSTITUTIONS
	CREDIT CARDS
	LOAN SERVICERS
	LAW OFFICES
	PHYSICIAN OFFICES (PEOPLE AND PETS)
	PREVIOUS LANDLORD/MORTGAGE COMPANY
	DEPARTMENT OF MOTOR VEHICLES
	IRS/REVENUE AGENCY
	BOARD OF ELECTIONS
	SOCIAL SECURITY
	IMMIGRATION
	UTILITIES (WATER, POWER, INTERNET, ETC.)
	HOME SERVICES (GARDENER, CLEANING SERVICE, ETC.)
	INSURANCE (HEALTH, HOME, CAR, ETC.)
	SHOPPING/STREAMING SERVICES
	MAGAZINES/NEWSPAPERS/CATALOGS
	ALMA MATERS

REMEMBER

Don't forget to set up mail forwarding to your new address; in most places you can register
a change of address completely online. There may be a small fee for doing so but the convenience
is well worth it. This is a time when you are vulnerable to identity theft, so take the
extra precautions to minimize your risks.

We've Moved!

NAME

ADDRESS

NAME

ADDRESS

NAME

ADDRESS

NAME

ADDRESS

NAME

ADDRESS

PART II

The History of a Home

THE HISTORY OF A HOME

"A house is not a home unless it contains food and fire for the mind as well as the body."
—Benjamin Franklin (1706 –1790), writer, scientist, and Founding Father

NOW THAT YOU'VE FOUND YOUR NEW SPACE, get to know its history. Whether you have moved across the country or just to a different neighborhood in the same area, new discoveries are always waiting to be found!

Check out your new location's city hall or hall of records for a deep dive into state and city history and lore. But for an insider's perspective, check out the local historical society. Having an interest in the past of your new neighborhood is also a great way to meet your neighbors. They may have been on your block for five years or fifty years, but there's no doubt that both experiences can give you great insight into how your new community operates.

In drilling down to the story of your new home, you are bound to uncover some amazing anecdotes around how it came to be. The previous owners or tenants will be fantastic resources as you learn about all the experiences they had in the home, both good and maybe not so great. Don't be afraid to embrace the negative and the positive; the presence of both creates an authentically lived-in home.

As you settle in, the space will start to welcome you in its own way. You'll slowly take in every nook and cranny, every chip and knot, and the story of this home will reveal itself. The architectural choices paint a narrative of those who came before and you'll soon discover what you can do to add your personal touches to that narrative. In digging deeper, what will you find that may have been left behind? You may discover long-forgotten heirlooms, messages scrawled in the backs of closets, or maybe even some buried treasure you can put toward your future renovations.

State History

FORMERLY KNOWN AS

DATE FOUNDED

NOTABLE LOCALS

AS SEEN IN FILMS + BOOKS

URBAN LEGENDS + MYSTERIES

INTERESTING TIDBITS

City History

FORMERLY KNOWN AS

NOTABLE LOCALS

AS SEEN IN FILMS + BOOKS

URBAN LEGENDS + MYSTERIES

INTERESTING TIDBITS

Neighborhood History

DATE FOUNDED •...•

FORMERLY KNOWN AS

NOTABLE LOCALS

AS SEEN IN FILMS + BOOKS

URBAN LEGENDS + MYSTERIES

INTERESTING TIDBITS

FACT

Homeowners' associations (HOAs) and local historic preservation societies have legal authority to dictate what you can and cannot do to your home. If your home is a designated historic landmark, you may be required to only use period-specific building materials or hire specialized contractors who understand the nuances and have additional certifications to work on historic properties. Make sure you understand your local ordinances before proceeding with any major renovations, especially work that is visible from outside.

Street History

FORMERLY KNOWN AS

....

....

....

....

NOTABLE LOCALS

....

....

....

....

....

....

....

....

....

AS SEEN IN FILMS + BOOKS

....

....

....

....

....

....

....

URBAN LEGENDS + MYSTERIES

INTERESTING TIDBITS

House History

FORMERLY KNOWN AS

....

....

....

....

NOTABLE RESIDENTS

....

....

....

....

....

....

....

....

....

AS SEEN IN FILMS + BOOKS

....

....

....

....

....

....

....

URBAN LEGENDS + MYSTERIES

INTERESTING TIDBITS

The Architectural Journey

YEAR ORIGINAL STRUCTURE BUILT

....

YEAR(S) OF NEW CONSTRUCTION

ARCHITECT(S)

....

....

....

....

BUILDER(S)/CONSTRUCTION FIRM(S)

....

....

STYLE

....

....

....

....

....

....

NOTABLE CHARACTERISTICS

....
....
....
....

ADDITIONS + RENOVATIONS

....
....
....
....
....
....
....

INTERESTING FACTS ABOUT THE SITE + PROPERTY

....
....
....
....
....

TIP

Have beadboard or wainscoting in your home? Modernize these classic
favorites by painting the drywall and boards different colors or using
a wallpaper on the top part.

Heirlooms + Hidden Treasures

HISTORICAL PERMANENT FEATURES

FOUND OBJECTS

HIDDEN SPACES

GHOST STORIES + LORE

Welcome Home

WELCOME HOME

"There is nothing like staying at home for real comfort."
—Jane Austen (1775 –1817), English novelist

UNDERSTANDING THE JOURNEY OF YOUR HOME so far is an important first step in setting up your space's future. You and the experiences you'll have in your home are the next layer in a storied history that someone else will look back on fondly one day, just as you have.

In this section, you'll record all the amazing memories from your time in this home. When you have your housewarming, invite your guests to make their mark in the guestbook. This is a simple way to hold everyone's information in one location for easy access later, but it's also helpful when it comes to sending thank-you cards for all the thoughtful gifts everyone will bring.

As the days pass, you'll get to know your home and the surrounding areas. Note down your favorite local spots as you discover them, as well as everything that makes your home unique, from sounds and smells to what comes and goes with the seasons.

This section also serves as the place to write down all your cherished family recipes. These can include those passed down through the generations and ones that you create in your new space. You can also record your favorite go-to meals for weekends, potlucks, brunches, drinks, and desserts.

Finally, take note of all the memorable moments you have in your home. The good and bad, the sad or funny, every experience is important and goes into what makes a home unique to you. These should also include all the holidays and celebrations you host at your home, so be sure to record all the moments from those days and any new traditions you start.

Housewarming Guest Book

NAME(S)   DATE

....

....

GIFT(S)

....

MESSAGE

....

....

NAME(S)   DATE

....

....

GIFT(S)

....

MESSAGE

....

....

....

NAME(S)   DATE

....

....

GIFT(S)

....

MESSAGE

....

....

....

NAME(S)   DATE

GIFT(S)

MESSAGE

NAME(S)   DATE

GIFT(S)

MESSAGE

NAME(S)   DATE

GIFT(S)

MESSAGE

Housewarming Guest Book

NAME(S) DATE

GIFT(S)

MESSAGE

NAME(S) DATE

GIFT(S)

MESSAGE

NAME(S) DATE

GIFT(S)

MESSAGE

NAME(S)

DATE

GIFT(S)

MESSAGE

NAME(S)

DATE

GIFT(S)

MESSAGE

NAME(S)

DATE

GIFT(S)

MESSAGE

Housewarming Guest Book

NAME(S)   DATE

....

....

GIFT(S)

....

MESSAGE

....

....

NAME(S)   DATE

....

....

GIFT(S)

....

MESSAGE

....

....

....

NAME(S)   DATE

....

....

GIFT(S)

....

MESSAGE

....

....

....

NAME(S)

DATE

GIFT(S)

MESSAGE

NAME(S)

DATE

GIFT(S)

MESSAGE

NAME(S)

DATE

GIFT(S)

MESSAGE

Housewarming Guest Book

NAME(S)   DATE

....

....

GIFT(S)

....

MESSAGE

....

....

NAME(S)   DATE

....

....

GIFT(S)

....

MESSAGE

....

....

NAME(S)   DATE

....

....

GIFT(S)

....

MESSAGE

....

....

NAME(S)   DATE
....

....

GIFT(S)
....

MESSAGE
....

....

NAME(S)   DATE
....

....

GIFT(S)
....

MESSAGE
....

....

....

NAME(S)   DATE
....

....

GIFT(S)
....

MESSAGE
....

....

....

Local Favorites: Food + Beverage

DATE	NAME	FAVORITE PARTS

REVISIT Y/N	NOTES

Local Favorites: Art + Culture

DATE	NAME	FAVORITE PARTS

REVISIT Y/N	NOTES

Local Favorites: Sports + Recreation

DATE	NAME	FAVORITE PARTS

REVISIT Y/N	NOTES

Local Favorites: Shopping

DATE	NAME	FAVORITE PARTS

REVISIT Y/N	NOTES

Local Favorites: Spiritual Places

DATE	NAME	FAVORITE PARTS

REVISIT Y/N	NOTES

Local Favorites: The Great Outdoors

DATE	NAME	FAVORITE PARTS

REVISIT Y/N	NOTES

Local Favorites: Historical Sightseeing

DATE	NAME	FAVORITE PARTS

REVISIT Y/N	NOTES

A Journey of Firsts

FIRST DAY

FIRST NIGHT

FIRST MEAL

FIRST VISITORS

FIRST NEIGHBORS MET

FIRST BIG PARTY

FIRST HOME PROJECT

FIRST SPOOKY MOMENT

A Journey of Firsts

FIRST BIG DÉCOR PURCHASE

FIRST TIME EXPLORING THE NEIGHBORHOOD

FIRST DATE NIGHT IN TOWN

FIRST REPAIR NEEDED

FIRST BIRTHDAY

FIRST ANNIVERSARY

Family Recipes

INGREDIENTS | TOOLS

INSTRUCTIONS

RECIPE NAME:

INGREDIENTS	TOOLS

INSTRUCTIONS

Family Recipes

INGREDIENTS	TOOLS

INSTRUCTIONS

RECIPE NAME:

INGREDIENTS	TOOLS

INSTRUCTIONS

Family Recipes

RECIPE NAME:

INGREDIENTS	TOOLS

INSTRUCTIONS

RECIPE NAME:

INGREDIENTS	TOOLS

INSTRUCTIONS

Family Recipes

RECIPE NAME:

INGREDIENTS	TOOLS

INSTRUCTIONS

RECIPE NAME:

INGREDIENTS	TOOLS

INSTRUCTIONS

Family Recipes

INGREDIENTS	TOOLS

INSTRUCTIONS

RECIPE NAME:

INGREDIENTS	TOOLS

INSTRUCTIONS

Favorite Meal Plans

MEAL PLAN 1

PANTRY STAPLES

MEAL PLAN 2

PANTRY STAPLES

Favorite Meal Plans

MEAL PLAN 3

PANTRY STAPLES

MEAL PLAN 4

PANTRY STAPLES

Favorite Meal Plans

MEAL PLAN 5

PANTRY STAPLES

MEAL PLAN 6

PANTRY STAPLES

Favorite Meal Plans

MEAL PLAN 7

PANTRY STAPLES

MEAL PLAN 8

PANTRY STAPLES

Favorite Meal Plans

MEAL PLAN 9

PANTRY STAPLES

MEAL PLAN 10

PANTRY STAPLES

Sounds + Smells

SMELLS UNIQUE TO YOUR HOME

Seasonal Observations: Spring

COLOR PALETTE

_____

_____

_____

_____

_____

HOME DÉCOR SWITCH-UP

_____

_____

_____

_____

_____

WEATHER + TEMPERATURE

_____

_____

_____

_____

_____

SMELLS OF THE SEASON

_____

_____

_____

_____

_____

CELESTIAL EVENTS

....
....
....
....
....

ANIMAL SIGHTINGS

....
....
....
....
....

LANDSCAPE + TERRAIN CHANGES

....
....
....
....
....
....
....
....
....
....
....
....
....

Seasonal Observations: Summer

COLOR PALETTE

HOME DÉCOR SWITCH-UP

WEATHER + TEMPERATURE

SMELLS OF THE SEASON

CELESTIAL EVENTS

_____

_____

_____

_____

_____

ANIMAL SIGHTINGS

_____

_____

_____

_____

_____

LANDSCAPE + TERRAIN CHANGES

_____

_____

_____

_____

_____

_____

DID YOU KNOW?

You can easily bring your home through the seasons by swapping out throw pillows, blankets, scented elements, and faux foliage to match the time of year. For example, spring and summer align with linens and greenery, while autumn and winter beg for cozy knits and wood features.

Seasonal Observations: Autumn

COLOR PALETTE

HOME DÉCOR SWITCH-UP

WEATHER + TEMPERATURE

SMELLS OF THE SEASON

CELESTIAL EVENTS

ANIMAL SIGHTINGS

LANDSCAPE + TERRAIN CHANGES

Seasonal Observations: Winter

COLOR PALETTE

....
....
....
....
....

HOME DÉCOR SWITCH-UP

....
....
....
....
....

WEATHER + TEMPERATURE

....
....
....
....
....

SMELLS OF THE SEASON

....
....
....
....
....

CELESTIAL EVENTS

....

....

....

....

....

ANIMAL SIGHTINGS

....

....

....

....

....

LANDSCAPE + TERRAIN CHANGES

....

....

....

....

....

....

TIP

Committing to a pattern plus the intimidating installation process can turn anyone off to the idea of using wallpaper. Thankfully, we now have removable wallpaper (think elevated contact paper) in many unique prints and textures, so you can change your mind as many times as you want and keep up with the trends too! And, since it's not a permanent option, it's a great option for renters.

Memorable Moments

THE GOOD	THE BAD

THE UGLY	THE UNFORGETTABLE

Memorable Moments

THE GOOD	THE BAD

THE UGLY	THE UNFORGETTABLE

Holidays + Celebrations

OCCASION

GUESTS

WHAT'S ON THE MENU

DECORATIONS

TRADITIONS

PLAYLIST

FAVORS

GIFT LIST FOR THANK-YOU NOTES

Holidays + Celebrations

OCCASION

GUESTS

WHAT'S ON THE MENU

DECORATIONS

TRADITIONS

PLAYLIST

FAVORS

GIFT LIST FOR THANK-YOU NOTES

Holidays + Celebrations

OCCASION

GUESTS

WHAT'S ON THE MENU

DECORATIONS

TRADITIONS

PLAYLIST

FAVORS

GIFT LIST FOR THANK-YOU NOTES

Holidays + Celebrations

OCCASION

GUESTS

WHAT'S ON THE MENU

DECORATIONS

TRADITIONS

PLAYLIST

FAVORS

GIFT LIST FOR THANK-YOU NOTES

Holidays + Celebrations

OCCASION

GUESTS

WHAT'S ON THE MENU

DECORATIONS

TRADITIONS

PLAYLIST

FAVORS

GIFT LIST FOR THANK-YOU NOTES

PART IV

Creating
Your Space

CREATING YOUR SPACE

> *"A house is made of walls and beams;*
> *a home is built with love and dreams."*
> —Ralph Waldo Emerson (1803 –1882),
> American essayist, lecturer, and poet

TO SAY THAT YOUR HOME IS YOUR SANCTUARY is no small statement. It's your retreat, your safe space, where you keep your most loved and treasured people and things. Because your home should comfort and welcome you, it's no surprise that this space would reflect who you and your family are. It should include all your favorite things, have an ambiance that sparks joy, and be functional for your needs.

The following section covers one of the best parts of home ownership—shopping! More specifically, space planning and designing. In most cases you are only restricted by the size of your space, but otherwise the sky is the limit when it comes to color palettes, textiles, and furniture styles. Maybe you prefer your space to be uniform and so use the same colors and themes throughout, or perhaps you are more eclectic and want to feel something different in every room. No matter your style, the most important thing is that your space works for you. You're not styling for anyone but you and your family. And remember, design and functionality can absolutely exist in harmony together, so don't allow yourself to be convinced that you must choose one or the other. It might take a little more effort and research, but you will find the perfect piece that ticks all the boxes!

The exterior of your home is just as important as your interior. Whether you have the room to make the outdoors an additional living space or you're just working with the front door of an apartment, the exterior is the first thing you and visitors see, so make sure to show it some love.

Once you have your layout and design exactly the way you want it, you'll need to maintain it so you can continue to enjoy your space for years to come. Take advantage of the home maintenance checklists for both interior and exterior. They are organized by season and can include everything from a schedule for winterizing your garden beds to the exact day to change over your décor accents from summer to autumn.

Room/Space

Purpose/Use	
Square Footage	
Wall Treatment	
Ceiling Treatment	
Floor Material	
Lighting Plan	
Special Features	
Mood/Vibe	
View(s)	

Room/Space

Purpose/Use	
Square Footage	
Wall Treatment	
Ceiling Treatment	
Floor Material	
Lighting Plan	
Special Features	
Mood/Vibe	
View(s)	

Room/Space

Purpose/Use

Square Footage

Wall Treatment

Ceiling
Treatment

Floor Material

Lighting Plan

Special Features

Mood/Vibe

View(s)

Room/Space ....

Purpose/Use	
Square Footage	
Wall Treatment	
Ceiling Treatment	
Floor Material	
Lighting Plan	
Special Features	
Mood/Vibe	
View(s)	

Room/Space ....

Purpose/Use	
Square Footage	
Wall Treatment	
Ceiling Treatment	
Floor Material	
Lighting Plan	
Special Features	
Mood/Vibe	
View(s)	

Room/Space

Purpose/Use	
Square Footage	
Wall Treatment	
Ceiling Treatment	
Floor Material	
Lighting Plan	
Special Features	
Mood/Vibe	
View(s)	

Room/Space

Purpose/Use	
Square Footage	
Wall Treatment	
Ceiling Treatment	
Floor Material	
Lighting Plan	
Special Features	
Mood/Vibe	
View(s)	

Room/Space

Purpose/Use	
Square Footage	
Wall Treatment	
Ceiling Treatment	
Floor Material	
Lighting Plan	
Special Features	
Mood/Vibe	
View(s)	

Floor Plan

Floor Plan

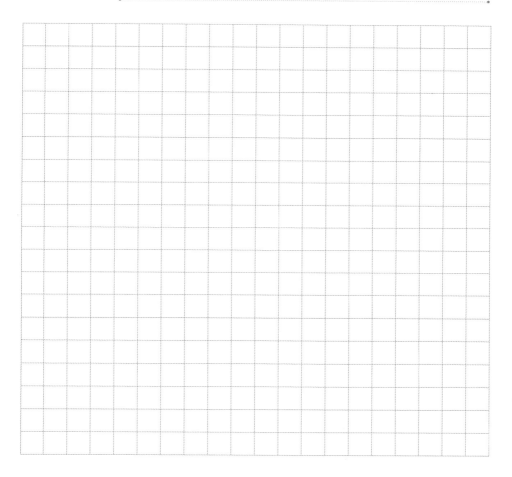

REMEMBER

Before you take a sledgehammer to any walls,
confirm 100 percent (usually via a structural engineer) which
walls are load bearing and should not be removed without
adding the proper support.

Floor Plan

Floor Plan

Floor Plan

Floor Plan

Floor Plan

Floor Plan

Mood Board

Notes

Mood Board

Notes

Mood Board

Notes

Mood Board

Notes

Paint + Wallpaper Record

Wall(s)		
Baseboard(s)		
Trim		
Molding(s)		
Ceiling		
Floor		
Window Casing(s)		
Door(s)		

INTERIOR

Paint + Wallpaper Record

Wall(s)		
Baseboard(s)		
Trim		
Molding(s)		
Ceiling		
Floor		
Window Casing(s)		
Door(s)		

Paint + Wallpaper Record

Wall(s)		
Baseboard(s)		
Trim		
Molding(s)		
Ceiling		
Floor		
Window Casing(s)		
Door(s)		

Paint + Wallpaper Record

Wall(s)

Baseboard(s)

Trim

Molding(s)

Ceiling

Floor

Window
Casing(s)

Door(s)

Shopping List for

Shopping List for ....

- ....
....

- ....
....

- ....
....

- ....
....

- ....
....

- ....
....

- ....
....

- ....

- ....

FACT

Paint samples (the little pots) use a special type of base formula. So even if your sample says eggshell, it's not the formula you will get if you buy a gallon of eggshell. The samples are strictly for color only.

Shopping List for

-
-
-
-
-
-
-
-
-

Shopping List for

-
-
-
-
-
-
-
-

Shopping List for ....

-
-
-
-
-
-
-
-
-

Shopping List for

-

-

-

-

-

-

-

-

-

Shopping List for

-

-

-

-

-

-

-

-

-

Shopping List for

-
-
-
-
-
-
-
-
-

Favorite Shops + Design Resources

PAINT + WALLPAPER	HARDWARE + LUMBER	ENTERTAINING + HOSTING	LIGHTING FIXTURES

ART + DÉCOR	FURNITURE	PLUMBING FIXTURES	TEXTILES + FABRICS

FACT

Everyone has heard of Carrara marble, but what about its cousin, Calacatta? The veins (or lines) in Carrara tend to be straighter and thinner, while Calacatta veins are much larger and thicker, and the white part of the marble is brighter. Calacatta is also rarer than Carrara, which is good to know if you want to go a more unique and special route in your design plans.

Home Maintenance Checklist: Spring

	CHANGE BATTERIES IN SMOKE/CARBON MONOXIDE DETECTORS
	CLEAN DRYER DUCTS
	CLEAN REFRIGERATOR COILS
	CLEAN RANGE HOOD/KITCHEN EXHAUST FAN
	CLEAN OVEN (INTERNAL)
	CLEAN KITCHEN WALLS, CABINETS
	CLEAN DISHWASHER SCREEN (FOOD PARTICLE CATCHER)
	CLEAN WASHING MACHINE FILTER
	FLUSH WATER HEATER
	CHECK DOORS/WINDOWS FOR WEAR, LUBRICATE MOVING PARTS
	CLEAN BASEBOARDS
	ROTATE MATTRESSES
	CLEAN HUMIDIFIERS
	WASH CURTAINS
	CLEAN/INSPECT CHIMNEY/FLUE
	RUN WATER AND FLUSH TOILETS IN UNUSED SPACES
	INSPECT AND REPLACE HVAC FILTERS

NOTE Every home and every homeowner is different, so these are recommendations, not rules. Please amend per your individual needs and consult and hire professionals as needed.

Home Maintenance Checklist: Summer

	CHECK SINKS, SHOWERS, TOILETS, TUBS FOR LEAKS
	TOUCH UP WALL/TRIM PAINT
	REPAIR WINDOW/DOOR CAULK AND WEATHER STRIPPING
	CLEAN GROUT IN ANY TILED AREAS
	SANITIZE AC DRAIN LINE
	INSPECT AND LUBRICATE GARAGE DOORS
	INSPECT/REPLACE INSULATION IN ATTICS, CRAWL SPACES
	PLUG HOLES, SPRAY PESTICIDE ON INSIDE PERIMETER
	CLEAN CEILING FANS
	RUN WATER AND FLUSH TOILETS IN UNUSED SPACES
	INSPECT AND REPLACE HVAC FILTERS

TIP

Consider an organic and/or environmentally friendly
pesticide over the typical name brand variety; the latter
almost always contain questionable chemicals that
could be harmful to you and your pets.

Home Maintenance Checklist: Autumn

	CHANGE BATTERIES IN SMOKE/CARBON MONOXIDE DETECTORS
	CLEAN DRYER DUCTS
	CLEAN REFRIGERATOR COILS
	CLEAN RANGE HOOD/KITCHEN EXHAUST FAN
	CHECK DOORS/WINDOWS FOR WEAR, LUBRICATE MOVING PARTS
	INSPECT FURNACE/AC
	CLEAN DISHWASHER SCREEN (FOOD PARTICLE CATCHER)
	CLEAN WASHING MACHINE FILTER
	CLEAN FAUCET AERATORS
	FLUSH WATER HEATER
	CLEAN HVAC DUCTS
	TEST GFCI/GFI OUTLETS
	ROTATE MATTRESSES
	INSPECT AND REPLACE HVAC FILTERS

FACT

It's important (and required by code in many countries, including the US!) to have ground fault circuit interrupter outlets (GFCIs or GFIs) in areas that could be exposed to water, such as kitchens, bathrooms, and basements. These outlets are specifically designed to protect against electrocution while using devices in wet areas.

Home Maintenance Checklist: Winter

	INSPECT/REPLACE INSULATION IN ATTICS, CRAWL SPACES
	PLUG ANY DRAFTY WINDOWS, DOORS
	BRING FIRE EXTINGUISHERS UP TO DATE
	REPLACE BATTERIES IN EMERGENCY ITEMS (RADIOS, FLASHLIGHTS)
	REPLENISH EMERGENCY CANDLES, MATCHES
	TEST GARAGE DOOR AUTO-REVERSE FEATURE
	RUN WATER AND FLUSH TOILETS IN UNUSED SPACES
	REFRESH PANTRY, DISCARD EXPIRED CANNED GOODS
	INSPECT AND REPLACE HVAC FILTERS
	RUN WATER AND FLUSH TOILETS IN UNUSED SPACES
	WINTERIZE UNCONDITIONED SPACES TO GUARD AGAINST FREEZING PIPES
	CHECK/REPLACE WASHING MACHINE WATER SUPPLY LINES

NOTE Every home and every homeowner is different, so these are recommendations, not rules. Please amend per your individual needs and consult and hire professionals as needed.

Features

STRUCTURES

HARDSCAPES

SOFTSCAPES

UNIQUE CHARACTERISTICS

Wish List

-

-

-

-

-

-

-

-

Mood Board

Notes

Paint + Materials Record

Retaining Wall(s)		
Fence/Gate		
Siding		
Doors/Windows		
Walkway(s)		
Driveway/Parking		
Roof/Gutters		
Brickwork		

Shopping List for

-
-
-
-
-
-
-
-
-

Shopping List for

-
-
-
-
-
-
-
-
-

Favorite Shops + Design Resources

PAINT + BUILDING MATERIALS	TOOLS + APPLIANCES	OUTDOOR ENTERTAINING	LIGHTING

DÉCOR	WATER FEATURES	GREENHOUSE	FURNITURE

DID YOU KNOW?

Just because a certain item is sold out in stores doesn't mean that is the end of the search. On resell sites like eBay, Poshmark, Mercari, and Apt Deco, you can find deals on pre-loved or never-been-opened items. Plus, shopping through these sites helps extend the life of these goods by keeping them out of landfills. So not only are you getting a great deal on something to enhance your home, but you're also helping out the environment.

Landscaping Plan: Front

Landscaping Plan: Back

Garden Planner: Front

Plant(s)		
Location		
Light/Shade		
Feeding		
Watering		
Pruning		
Pest Protection		
Winterizing		
Other		

Garden Planner: Back

Home Maintenance Checklist: Spring

	UNCOVER AC CONDENSER
	CLEAN GUTTERS AND CHECK DOWNSPOUTS
	PRESSURE WASH EXTERIOR AND WALKWAYS
	INSPECT/REPAIR BRICK AND MORTAR
	INSPECT/REPAIR FOUNDATION FOR CRACKS AND LEAKS
	INSPECT/REPAIR WALKWAYS FOR CRACKS
	TURN ON EXTERIOR WATER
	CHECK WATER DRAINAGE/GRADING FROM DOWNSPOUTS TO THE STREET
	PRUNE OVERGROWTH IN PUBLIC-FACING WALKWAYS

TIP

Having maintenance checklists for each season spreads out the work over the year so it becomes more manageable and allows you to stay on top of the condition of your home. Some things, like gutters, should be checked four times a year for proper operation, but maybe only need cleaning during the autumn months.

Home Maintenance Checklist: Summer

	CLEAN GUTTERS AND CHECK DOWNSPOUTS
	CHECK ROOF FOR LEAKS, PATCH SHINGLES
	TOUCH UP PAINT ON SIDING, WINDOWS, AND TRIM
	CLEAN AND REPAIR DECK/PATIO
	KEEP UP WITH YARD AND TREE MAINTENANCE
	INSPECT/REPLACE GAS LINE FOR OUTSIDE APPLIANCES (GRILLS, COOKTOPS, ETC.)
	FILL PROPANE TANKS

NOTE Every home and every homeowner is different, so these are recommendations, not rules. Please amend per your individual needs and consult and hire professionals as needed.

Home Maintenance Checklist: Autumn

	CLEAN AND COVER AC CONDENSER
	CLEAN GUTTERS AND CHECK DOWNSPOUTS
	WASH EXTERIOR WINDOWS
	INSPECT/REPAIR BRICK AND MORTAR
	INSPECT/REPAIR FOUNDATION FOR CRACKS AND LEAKS
	CLEAN/STORE PATIO FURNITURE
	TURN OFF EXTERIOR WATER
	WINTERIZE PLANTS
	INSTALL STORM WINDOWS

NOTE Every home and every homeowner is different, so these are recommendations, not rules. Please amend per your individual needs and consult and hire professionals as needed.

Home Maintenance Checklist: Winter

	CLEAN GUTTERS AND CHECK DOWNSPOUTS
	CLEAR WALKWAYS OF SNOW/ICE (IF APPLICABLE)
	COVER OUTDOOR COOKING APPLIANCES

REMEMBER

Many maintenance items revolve around the management and containment of water throughout the year. Just staying on top of keeping water out of the places where it does not belong can go a long way toward maintaining the longevity of your home and extending the useful life and condition of your home's building materials.

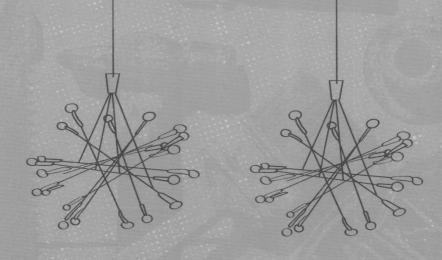

PART V

Projects in Progress

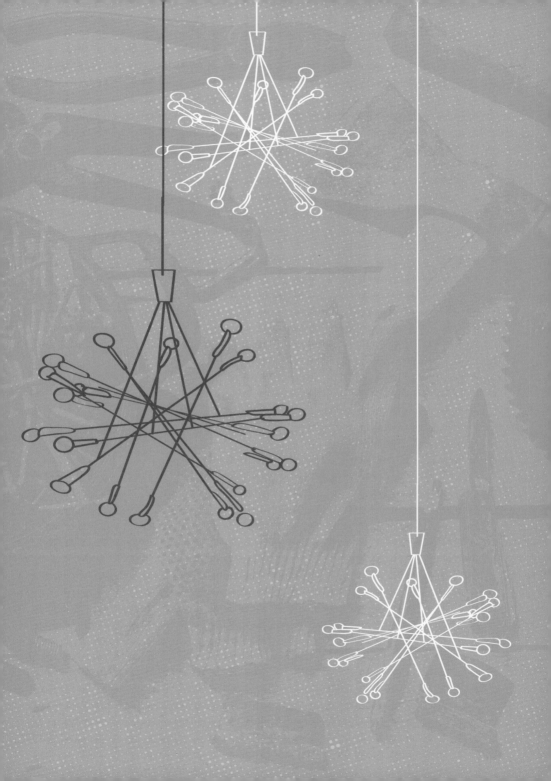

PROJECTS IN PROGRESS

"Strength of character may be learned at work, but beauty of character is learned at home."

—Henry Drummond (1851–1897), Scottish scientist, writer, and evangelist

THE PROJECTS NEVER END WHEN YOU'RE A HOMEOWNER. No truer words have ever been spoken. But that doesn't mean that your story of home design and maintenance can't be one of adventure and discovery. Of course, the larger projects that you take on for the sake of aesthetics will be full of excitement as you continue to tune and tweak this home to be your own. But joy and fulfillment can be found in every task, from the most mundane to the insanely complex. By replacing that leaky faucet or outdated electrical panel, you're protecting your family and making your home safe. In converting that dated 1960s galley kitchen into a family room, you've created a space where kids can be their messy, lawless selves and feel like they've made their mark (sometimes literally) on their home.

While DIY projects can be incredibly rewarding and fun, knowing when to call in the professionals is key. You know yourself and you know your limits and skills. Don't be a hero. Take the time to research design firms or contractors and hire a team you feel comfortable with, a crew that will fix and renovate your home with the same love and care that you would. Don't settle for anything less than that.

In the pages that follow, chart your progress on your projects, both large and small. Keep yourself on task with to-do lists for immediate upgrades and repairs, goals that can be accomplished over a long weekend, and loftier goals that may involve multiple months and a crew of some sort. And speaking of crews, there is also space for you to keep the details and price quotes of those who assist you along the way in seeing your visions come to life.

To-Do List: Immediate Fixes

PROJECT	
WHAT'S NEEDED	
TIMEFRAME	

PROJECT	
WHAT'S NEEDED	
TIMEFRAME	

PROJECT	
WHAT'S NEEDED	
TIMEFRAME	

PROJECT	
WHAT'S NEEDED	
TIMEFRAME	

PROJECT	
WHAT'S NEEDED	
TIMEFRAME	

PROJECT	
WHAT'S NEEDED	
TIMEFRAME	

PROJECT	
WHAT'S NEEDED	
TIMEFRAME	

REMEMBER

Paint is the easiest and most budget-friendly way to change the feel of a room. But it's okay to change your mind if you don't love it after a few days. With a little primer and a free weekend, you can try again and again until you are in love with your space completely.

To-Do List: Short-Term Fixes

PROJECT	
WHAT'S NEEDED	
TIMEFRAME	

PROJECT	
WHAT'S NEEDED	
TIMEFRAME	

PROJECT	
WHAT'S NEEDED	
TIMEFRAME	

PROJECT	
WHAT'S NEEDED	
TIMEFRAME	

To-Do List: Long-Term Fixes

PROJECT	
WHAT'S NEEDED	
TIMEFRAME	

PROJECT	
WHAT'S NEEDED	
TIMEFRAME	

PROJECT	
WHAT'S NEEDED	
TIMEFRAME	

PROJECT	
WHAT'S NEEDED	
TIMEFRAME	

Project

Problem

Solution

Sketch + Paste

Budget

Building Materials Needed

Styling Items to Buy

PROFESSIONAL CONTACTS

COMPANY	CONTACT NAME
PHONE + EMAIL	
QUOTE FOR SERVICES	

COMPANY	CONTACT NAME
PHONE + EMAIL	
QUOTE FOR SERVICES	

COMPANY	CONTACT NAME
PHONE + EMAIL	
QUOTE FOR SERVICES	

COMPANY	CONTACT NAME
PHONE + EMAIL	
QUOTE FOR SERVICES	

STEP-BY-STEP PLAN	TIMELINE

ACTIVITY LOG	NOTES + REFERENCES

TIP For small projects, like painting a side table or creating a design on a feature wall, feel free to use leftover paint sample pots. However, because the formula used for samples is not the same as you will get with gallons, don't use samples on things like walls or doors in high-traffic areas that need to stand the test of time.

Project

Problem

Solution

Sketch + Paste

Budget

_____

_____

Building Materials Needed

_____

_____

Styling Items to Buy

_____

_____

_____

PROFESSIONAL CONTACTS

COMPANY	CONTACT NAME
PHONE + EMAIL	
QUOTE FOR SERVICES	

COMPANY	CONTACT NAME
PHONE + EMAIL	
QUOTE FOR SERVICES	

COMPANY	CONTACT NAME
PHONE + EMAIL	
QUOTE FOR SERVICES	

COMPANY	CONTACT NAME
PHONE + EMAIL	
QUOTE FOR SERVICES	

STEP-BY-STEP PLAN	TIMELINE

ACTIVITY LOG	NOTES + REFERENCES

FACT

The term *accent wall* has been replaced by *feature wall* or *statement wall* to encourage homeowners to offset their spaces with more than just paint. Wallpaper, a gallery wall, an art installation, or a textured wall are all possibilities!

Project

Problem

Solution

Sketch + Paste

Budget

Building Materials Needed

Styling Items to Buy

PROFESSIONAL CONTACTS	
COMPANY	CONTACT NAME
PHONE + EMAIL	
QUOTE FOR SERVICES	

COMPANY	CONTACT NAME
PHONE + EMAIL	
QUOTE FOR SERVICES	

COMPANY	CONTACT NAME
PHONE + EMAIL	
QUOTE FOR SERVICES	

COMPANY	CONTACT NAME
PHONE + EMAIL	
QUOTE FOR SERVICES	

STEP-BY-STEP PLAN	TIMELINE

ACTIVITY LOG	NOTES + REFERENCES

TIP

Invest in a mini tape measure, one that can always be kept in your bag or car and can go with you on outings to hardware and home goods stores. Measuring for your space in real time will save you from having to do returns later!

Project

Problem

Solution

Sketch + Paste

Budget

Building Materials Needed

Styling Items to Buy

PROFESSIONAL CONTACTS	
COMPANY	CONTACT NAME
PHONE + EMAIL	
QUOTE FOR SERVICES	

COMPANY	CONTACT NAME
PHONE + EMAIL	
QUOTE FOR SERVICES	

COMPANY	CONTACT NAME
PHONE + EMAIL	
QUOTE FOR SERVICES	

COMPANY	CONTACT NAME
PHONE + EMAIL	
QUOTE FOR SERVICES	

STEP-BY-STEP PLAN	TIMELINE

ACTIVITY LOG	NOTES + REFERENCES

TIP

Love whitewash wood but don't want to fully replace floors or a piece of furniture? Create it yourself using a gray paint base and watered-down white paint on top for an antique, weathered look. Apply with your choice of tool—brush, sponge, or rag—to achieve your desired level of distressed style.

Project

Problem

Solution

Sketch + Paste

Budget

....

....

Building Materials Needed

....

....

Styling Items to Buy

....

....

....

....

PROFESSIONAL CONTACTS

COMPANY	CONTACT NAME
PHONE + EMAIL	
QUOTE FOR SERVICES	

COMPANY	CONTACT NAME
PHONE + EMAIL	
QUOTE FOR SERVICES	

COMPANY	CONTACT NAME
PHONE + EMAIL	
QUOTE FOR SERVICES	

COMPANY	CONTACT NAME
PHONE + EMAIL	
QUOTE FOR SERVICES	

STEP-BY-STEP PLAN	TIMELINE

Inner Workings

INNER WORKINGS

"It takes a heap o' livin' in a house t' make it home."
—Edgar Albert Guest (1881–1959), English-born American poet

AFTER PUTTING SO MUCH LOVE AND CARE into creating the best space possible for you and your family, you want to ensure that it remains safe and protected. The best way to do this is to keep the inner workings of your home organized and running smoothly. These details are not necessarily glamorous, but they are absolutely necessary, and keeping them up to date and in one central location will make for easy reference when or if an unfortunate event occurs.

Having a running list of your possessions is vital when it comes to insurance claims. You want to be as specific as possible and include makes and models of appliances and electronics, as well as the true value of clothes, shoes, and jewelry. Similarly, recording the layout of your property complete with measurements and structure sketches will be helpful if any neighbor or city disputes arise. When purchasing a home, make sure you get a copy of the site survey from the title company; you can paste it in this section for safekeeping.

Keeping tabs on the monetary output of your home can also help it run efficiently. Seeing all your expenses month to month can help you identify where you might be overspending so you can shop around for a better price and provider. Noting payments can also show areas where you might be able to cut back if you want to start saving for a new renovation or vacation.

In this section there is also space for you to note down important contact information for contractors, repair personnel, key neighbors, and emergency services. In times of high stress or crisis, you'll be happy you thought ahead to keep such important information stored in an easy-to-locate and convenient place.

Insurance Inventory

-
-
-
-
-
-
-
-
-
-
-
-
-

-
-
-
-
-
-
-
-
-
-
-
-
-

-
-
-
-
-
-
-
-
-
-

-
-
-
-
-
-
-
-
-
-

TIP

Be detailed when making your inventory. The difference between "Toaster" and "Breville BOV800XL Smart Oven Convection Toaster Oven, Brushed Stainless Steel" can be several hundred dollars during the claims process when you need it most.

Property Lines + Site Survey

NOTES

NOTES

....

....

....

....

FACT

In many cities, the sidewalks in front of your property are not technically yours, but you are responsible for their maintenance and liable to the general public for safe usage throughout the year (think ice and snow removal, crack repairs, and other similar instances).

Monthly Payments

	JAN	FEB	MAR	APR	MAY
MORTGAGE					
PROPERTY TAX					
PROPERTY INSURANCE					
VEHICLE INSURANCE/ REGISTRATION					
HEALTH/DENTAL INSURANCE					
HOA FEES					
GARBAGE/RECYCLING					
LANDSCAPING					
WATER					
ELECTRICITY					
GAS/OIL					
INTERNET					
STREAMING SERVICES					
PEST CONTROL SERVICES					
CREDIT CARDS					
STUDENT/OTHER LOANS					
PET GROOMING/ MEDICATIONS					
TUITION/EDUCATION					
GYM/EXERCISE CLASSES + SUBSCRIPTIONS					

JUN	JUL	AUG	SEPT	OCT	NOV	DEC

Contractor + Repair Contacts

COMPANY

CONTACT NAME

ADDRESS

QUOTE FOR SERVICES

WORK COMPLETED

PHONE   EMAIL

COMPANY

CONTACT NAME

ADDRESS

QUOTE FOR SERVICES

WORK COMPLETED

PHONE   EMAIL

COMPANY

CONTACT NAME

ADDRESS

QUOTE FOR SERVICES

WORK COMPLETED

PHONE   EMAIL

COMPANY

CONTACT NAME

ADDRESS

QUOTE FOR SERVICES

WORK COMPLETED

PHONE   EMAIL

COMPANY

CONTACT NAME

ADDRESS

QUOTE FOR SERVICES

WORK COMPLETED

PHONE   EMAIL

NOTES

TIP

Finding quality contractors is hard. When you find a good one, hold on to their contact information and spread the word to friends and neighbors. Word of mouth is how all the good contractors regularly find work, because they don't need to advertise.

Utilities + Service Providers

COMPANY

SERVICE PLAN/ACCOUNT NUMBER

NOTES

PHONE   EMAIL

COMPANY

SERVICE PLAN/ACCOUNT NUMBER

NOTES

PHONE   EMAIL

COMPANY

SERVICE PLAN/ACCOUNT NUMBER

NOTES

PHONE   EMAIL

COMPANY

SERVICE PLAN/ACCOUNT NUMBER

NOTES

PHONE   EMAIL

COMPANY

SERVICE PLAN/ACCOUNT NUMBER

NOTES

PHONE   EMAIL

COMPANY

SERVICE PLAN/ACCOUNT NUMBER

NOTES

PHONE   EMAIL

COMPANY

SERVICE PLAN/ACCOUNT NUMBER

NOTES

PHONE   EMAIL

COMPANY

SERVICE PLAN/ACCOUNT NUMBER

NOTES

PHONE   EMAIL

NOTES

TIP

Set up utilities in advance so everything is ready on move-in day.
Most utility companies allow you to set a start date weeks
or even months in advance.

Appliances + Systems

APPLIANCE/SYSTEM

MODEL + SERIAL NUMBER

WARRANTY INFORMATION

PURCHASE + INSTALLATION DATES

SERVICE DATES + NOTES

APPLIANCE/SYSTEM

MODEL + SERIAL NUMBER

WARRANTY INFORMATION

PURCHASE + INSTALLATION DATES

SERVICE DATES + NOTES

APPLIANCE/SYSTEM

MODEL + SERIAL NUMBER

WARRANTY INFORMATION

PURCHASE + INSTALLATION DATES

SERVICE DATES + NOTES

APPLIANCE/SYSTEM

MODEL + SERIAL NUMBER

WARRANTY INFORMATION

PURCHASE + INSTALLATION DATES

SERVICE DATES + NOTES

APPLIANCE/SYSTEM

MODEL + SERIAL NUMBER

WARRANTY INFORMATION

PURCHASE + INSTALLATION DATES

SERVICE DATES + NOTES

NOTES

TIP

It may be tempting to get a washer and dryer with all the fancy bells and whistles, but consider getting a simpler model. More features usually mean more things that can (and will) break. For all your appliances, try to stick with a major brand that has a good local support network for when you inevitably need repairs.

Safety + Security

ALARM COMPANY	**PHONE**
ALARM CODE	
CODE WORD FOR **"ALL OKAY"**	
CODE WORD FOR **"HELP NEEDED"**	
ACCOUNT NUMBER	
HARDWARE SERIAL NUMBERS	
EMAIL	

FIRE EXTINGUISHER
MANUFACTURER DATE
EXPIRATION DATE
NEXT SERVICE DUE DATE

SPARE KEY LOCATION(S)

EMERGENCY CONTACTS	
NEIGHBOR NAME	PHONE
EMAIL	
NEIGHBOR NAME	PHONE
EMAIL	
NEIGHBOR NAME	PHONE
EMAIL	

FIRE		PHONE	
POLICE		PHONE	
MEDICAL		PHONE	

EMERGENCY BAG COMPONENTS

REMEMBER
Test smoke and carbon monoxide
detectors monthly and replace batteries annually.

Conclusion

JUST LIKE YOUR CLOTHES OR HAIRSTYLE, your home has the potential to be a wonderful expression of your personal style and identity. From the type of architecture you find attractive to the color of the rug you place in your entryway, every piece of your home is infused with a little bit of you. The greatest compliment you can receive is when you invite over friends and family and they tell you that your space is "so you." (And that it smells good—candles will be your best friends.)

As time goes on, you will grow as a person. Your needs will change and your style will evolve, and so must your home grow with you. That might mean you do a complete refresh with new paint and décor and you change how certain rooms are used. But it could also mean you have to say goodbye to one space and kick off a brand-new adventure to find the next one. While it may be sad to leave, you are taking with you so many wonderful memories and lessons learned that you can revisit in your new space. Plus, you can start new traditions, which is nothing less than thrilling.

Remember, home is what you make it. Home is made by you.

About the Authors

THE KHALIGHIS ARE BAYAN AND CARA, a husband-and-wife duo from Philadelphia who have been renovating and designing spaces together on the East Coast since 2013.

Their current project, a mid-century split-level in New Jersey, has been undergoing its transformation since 2018, and is home to the couple and their beloved cats.

> *"Where we love is home—home that our feet may leave, but not our hearts."*
> —Oliver Wendell Holmes Sr. (1809–1894), American physician, professor, writer, and poet

Need additional templates? Scan below for printable versions of annual checklists and other fill-in sheets.

**MOVING
TO-DO LIST**

**PROJECT
PLANNER**

FAMILY RECIPES

**FAVORITE
MEAL PLANS**

**SEASONAL
OBSERVATIONS**

**INTERIOR
MAINTENANCE
CHECKLISTS**

EXTERIOR
MAINTENANCE
CHECKLISTS

**INSURANCE
INVENTORY**

**MONTHLY
PAYMENTS**

First published in 2023 by Wellfleet Press, an imprint of The Quarto Group,
142 West 36th Street, 4th Floor, New York, NY 10018, USA
T (212) 779-4972 F (212) 779-6058 www.Quarto.com

Wellfleet titles are also available at discount for retail, wholesale, promotional, and bulk purchase. For details, contact the Special Sales Manager by email at specialsales@quarto.com or by mail at The Quarto Group, Attn: Special Sales Manager, 100 Cummings Center Suite 265D, Beverly, MA 01915 USA.

10 9 8 7 6 5 4 3 2 1

ISBN: 978-1-57715-386-3

Group Publisher: Rage Kindelsperger
Creative Director: Laura Drew
Managing Editor: Cara Donaldson
Editor: Elizabeth You
Cover and Interior Design: Beth Middleworth
Text: Cara Donaldson and Bayan Khalighi

Printed in China

For entertainment purposes only. Do not attempt any project or construction discussed in this book without proper research and consulting or hiring a professional. The author, publisher, packager, manufacturer, distributor, and their collective agents waive all liability for the reader's use or application of any of the text herein. Use great caution when embarking on do-it-yourself projects or construction. Always wear the recommended safety gear and have a fire extinguisher at the ready.